# How To Use This Study Guide

I0177595

This five-lesson study guide corresponds to *"Speaking in Tongues — What Is It and Is It Really for Everyone?" With Rick Renner* (Renner TV). Each lesson in this study guide covers a topic that is addressed during the program series, with questions and references supplied to draw you deeper into your own private study of the Scriptures on this subject.

To derive the most benefit from this study guide, consider the following:

**First,** watch or listen to the program prior to working through the corresponding lesson in this guide. (Programs can also be viewed at **renner.org** by clicking on the Media/Archives links or on our Renner Ministries YouTube channel.)

**Second,** take the time to look up the scriptures included in each lesson. Prayerfully consider their application to your own life.

**Third,** use a journal or notebook to make note of your answers to each lesson's Study Questions and Practical Application challenges.

**Fourth,** invest specific time in prayer and in the Word of God to consult with the Holy Spirit. Write down the scriptures or insights He reveals to you.

**Finally,** take action! Whatever the Lord tells you to do according to His Word, do it.

For added insights on this subject, it is recommended that you obtain Rick Renner's books *The Holy Spirit and You: Working Together As Heaven's Dynamic Duo* and *Why We Need the Gifts of the Holy Spirit.* You may also select from Rick's other available resources, such as his book *Fallen Angels, Giants, Monsters, and the World Before the Flood,* by placing your order at **renner.org** or by calling 1-800-742-5593.

TOPIC

# The First Work of Grace

## SCRIPTURES

1. **John 20:19-22** — Then the same day at evening, being the first day of the week, when the doors were shut where the disciples were assembled for fear of the Jews, came Jesus and stood in the midst, and saith unto them, Peace be unto you. And when he had so said, he shewed unto them his hands and his side. Then were the disciples glad, when they saw the Lord. Then said Jesus to them again, Peace be unto you: as my Father hath sent me, even so send I you. And when he had said this, he breathed on them, and saith unto them, Receive ye the Holy Ghost.

2. **Genesis 2:7** — And the Lord God formed man of the dust of the ground, and breathed into his nostrils the breath of life; and man became a living soul.

3. **Ephesians 1:13,14** — In whom ye also trusted, after that ye heard the word of truth, the gospel of your salvation: in whom also after that ye believed, ye were sealed with that holy Spirit of promise, which is the earnest of our inheritance until the redemption of the purchased possession, unto the praise of his glory.

4. **Ephesians 2:10** — For we are his workmanship, created in Christ Jesus unto good works, which God hath before ordained that we should walk in them.

5. **Luke 24:49** — And, behold, I send the promise of my Father upon you: but tarry ye in the city of Jerusalem, until ye be endued with power from on high.

## GREEK WORDS

1. "breathed on them" — ἐμφυσάω (*emphusao*): to breathe into; to inflate

2. "receive" — Λάβετε (*labete*): to take right now; to actively receive

3. "breathed" — ἐμφυσάω (*emphusao*): to breathe into; to inflate

# A Note From Rick Renner

I am on a personal quest to see a "revival of the Bible" so people can establish their lives on a firm foundation that will stand strong and endure the test as end-time storm winds begin to intensify.

In order to experience a revival of the Bible in your personal life, it is important to take time each day to read, receive, and apply its truths to your life. James tells us that if we will continue in the perfect law of liberty — refusing to be forgetful hearers, but determined to be doers — we will be blessed in our ways. As you watch or listen to the programs in this series and work through this corresponding study guide, I trust you will search the Scriptures and allow the Holy Spirit to help you hear something new from God's Word that applies specifically to your life. I encourage you to be a doer of the Word He reveals to you. Whatever the cost, I assure you — it will be worth it.

> Thy words were found, and I did eat them;
> and thy word was unto me the joy and rejoicing of mine heart:
> for I am called by thy name, O Lord God of hosts.
> — Jeremiah 15:16

Your brother and friend in Jesus Christ,

Rick Renner

*Speaking in Tongues*
*What Is It and Is It Really for Everyone?*

Published by Rick Renner Ministries
www.renner.org

ISBN 13: 978-1-6675-0742-2

ISBN 13 eBook: 978-1-6675-0743-9

4. "sealed" — σφραγίζω (*sphragidzo*): pictures a seal placed on a package after the product had been thoroughly examined and inspected to make sure it was fully intact and complete; the seal was proof the product was impeccable; normally such seals bore the insignia of a wealthy or famous person, which meant that this package was to be treated with tender care; the seal affirmed who was the owner and guaranteed the package would make it to its final destination

5. "earnest" — ἀρραβών (*arrabon*): a payment given in advance to guarantee the whole amount will be paid afterward; earnest-money; an installment; a deposit; a down-payment which guarantees full delivery of a promise; security deposit given by the purchaser to assure confidence and peace to the seller that he will fulfill his promise

6. "workmanship" — ποίημα (*poiema*): a poem; a product; a literary masterpiece; a shiny piece of art

7. "created" — κτίζω (*ktidzo*): the creation of something from nothing

8. "behold" — ἰδού (*idou*): wow; look; see; a sense of amazement

9. "endued" — ἐνδύω (*enduo*): to be empowered; to clothe

10. "power" — δύναμις (*dunamis*): explosive, superhuman power with enormous energy that produces phenomenal, extraordinary, and unparalleled results; the force of an entire army; a force of nature, like an earthquake, hurricane, or tornado

## SYNOPSIS

The five lessons in this study titled *Speaking in Tongues — What Is It and Is It Really for Everyone?* will focus on the following topics:

- The First Work of Grace
- The Second Work of Grace
- Why Should You Speak in Tongues?
- The By-Product of the Baptism in the Holy Spirit
- Other Benefits of Being Filled With the Holy Spirit

What actually happens when a person first surrenders his or her life to God? What role does the Holy Spirit play? And what scriptures really help explain the extraordinary experience of being *born again* that Jesus spoke of in John 3? If you've ever had questions like these, this lesson will provide you with answers!

The emphasis of this lesson:

The first work of grace is salvation. It is the starting place of your new relationship with God through the Person of the Holy Spirit. The moment you repent of your sin and surrender your life to Christ, you are filled and sealed with the Holy Spirit. He washes you clean, and you become a brand-new creation in Christ Jesus.

## The Day Jesus' Disciples Got Saved

The very first record in the Bible of people getting "saved" is found in the gospel of John. Jesus had been crucified, and it was now the first day of the week and the disciples were hiding behind closed doors. They were afraid of what the Jewish leaders might do to them. It was at this point that something suddenly happened. Scripture says:

> Then the same day at evening, being the first day of the week, when the doors were shut where the disciples were assembled for fear of the Jews, came Jesus and stood in the midst, and saith unto them, Peace be unto you. And when he had so said, he shewed unto them his hands and his side. Then were the disciples glad, when they saw the Lord. Then said Jesus to them again, Peace be unto you: as my Father hath sent me, even so send I you. And when he had said this, he breathed on them, and saith unto them, Receive ye the Holy Ghost.
> — John 20:19-22

Notice that twice in these four verses, Jesus said, "Peace be with you." That is important as we will see a little later. Nevertheless, after speaking peace to them a second time, Jesus "breathed on them." In Greek, the phrase "breathed on them" is the word *emphusao*, which means *to breathe into* or *to inflate*. It is the word we would use to describe the process of blowing up a balloon. To inflate a balloon, we don't blow *on* it — we blow *into* it, and it receives our breath and is filled.

That is what took place when Jesus breathed into the disciples and said, "…Receive ye the Holy Ghost" (John 20:22). The word "receive" is the Greek word *labete*, which is a direct form of *lambano*, and it means *to take right now* or *to actively receive*. In that moment, Jesus literally breathed His Spirit into His disciples' spirit, and when the Holy Spirit entered them, they were all saved.

What's interesting is that in the Septuagint, which is the Greek version of the Old Testament, this same word for breathing into (*emphusao*) is used in the account of man's creation. The Bible says, "And the Lord God formed man of the dust of the ground, and *breathed* into his nostrils the breath of life; and man became a living soul" (Genesis 2:7). The word "breathed" here is the word *emphusao*, which means *to breathe into* or *to inflate*. It is the breath of God that animates a person's physical body and enables them to become a living soul.

Some people claim that when Jesus breathed on His disciples in John 20, He was just prophesying what was going to take place about 50 days later on the day of Pentecost, but that was not the case. It was right then and there — in the very moment when Jesus breathed on them — that the disciples were born again, and the Holy Spirit entered their lives. We know this to be the case because of the use of the word *labete* — the Greek word for "received," which means *to take something now, at that very moment*, and *to actively receive*.

# A Historic Moment

Up until that moment in history, the Spirit of God had never indwelt a person. Instead, when the Spirit interacted with someone, He always came *upon* them. We see throughout the Old Testament. For example, when Samson fought against the Philistines, the Bible says that the Spirit of God came upon him, and he was victorious (*see* Judges 14:19; 15:14). We find this was the case with Othniel, Gideon, and even King Saul (*see* Judges 3:9-11; 6:34; 1 Samuel 10:10). Once each person accomplished his assigned task, the Spirit of God would lift off him, and he would be reduced to an ordinary man once again.

But that was not the case with Jesus' disciples. When He breathed on them and said, "…Receive ye the Holy Ghost" (John 20:22), the Holy Spirit entered them and never left them! Indeed, this was a historic moment — for the very first time, the Spirit entered human hearts, and people became His temple (*see* 1 Corinthians 6:19). Again, the day Jesus breathed on His disciples to receive the Holy Spirit was the first documented record of people being born again.

# When You Got Saved,
# You Were 'Sealed' With the Holy Spirit

The moment the new birth in Christ takes place, many supernatural things take place. The apostle Paul speaks of this in his letter to the Ephesians. For example, in Ephesians 1:13, Paul wrote:

**In whom ye also trusted, after that ye heard the word of truth, the gospel of your salvation: in whom also after that ye believed, ye were sealed with that holy Spirit of promise.**

In this verse, the word "sealed" is very significant. It is the Greek word *sphragidzo*, and it pictures *a seal placed on a package after the product had been thoroughly examined and inspected to make sure it was fully intact and complete.* The seal was proof the product was impeccable. Normally, such seals bore the insignia of a wealthy or famous person, which meant that this package was to be treated with tender care. The seal also affirmed who was the owner and guaranteed the package would make it to its final destination.

The use of this word *sphragidzo* — translated here as "sealed" — means that when you were saved and the Holy Spirit came into you, God inspected you to make sure you were complete. Once He saw that you were a new creation in Christ and impeccable on the inside, He placed His seal of approval on you — the seal of His Spirit — as proof that your heart was flawless. The seal of His Spirit is also the guarantee that you're going to make it all the way to your heavenly destination.

When we factor in the original Greek meaning of the key words in this verse, the *Renner Interpretive Version* (*RIV*) of Ephesians 1:13 reads:

**When you were placed in Christ, God stamped you with a special seal and embossed it so deeply that it cannot be broken, erased, rubbed out, wiped out, deleted, or removed; that unbreakable seal is the Holy Spirit. Once you were stamped with Him, it meant you had God's approval. He examined the contents of your heart and found nothing flawed or inferior. And because everything was in order, He stamped you with the Holy Spirit, which is His seal of approval. Anyone who has this stamp is headed for special treatment. This seal means you belong to God and no one is to interfere with you as a**

"package." This "Holy Spirit stamp" means the postage is prepaid to get you all the way to your ultimate destination. That means you can be sure that once your journey with the Lord begins, you are going to make it all the way to where God wants you to go!

## The Holy Spirit Is God's Down-Payment To Show He's Serious About Your Salvation

In the very next verse, the apostle Paul goes on to explain that the deposit of the Holy Spirit into our lives "…is the earnest of our inheritance until the redemption of the purchased possession, unto the praise of his glory" (Ephesians 1:14).

The word "earnest" in this verse is the Greek word *arrabon*, and it describes *a payment given in advance to guarantee the whole amount will be paid afterward*. It is *earnest-money*, *an installment*, *a deposit*, or *a down-payment*, which guarantees full delivery of a promise. This word *arrabon* essentially depicts *a security deposit given by the purchaser to assure confidence and peace to the seller that he will fulfill his promise*.

When we factor in the original Greek meaning of the key words in this verse, the *Renner Interpretive Version* (*RIV*) of Ephesians 1:14 is as follows:

> As good as all of this already seems, it's only the beginning of all that God has planned for us! The Holy Spirit is just the first installment of the incredible things that God has planned as a part of our full inheritance. You might say the Holy Spirit is God's down-payment or "money down" to show that He is serious and intends to complete the deal, finalize all the papers, put the product in His name, and finally make us His very own possession, with no one else having the ability to exercise any claims or liens against us. When this process is finally wrapped up and the deal is completely sealed, we're all going to want to stand up and give God a round of applause for everything accomplished in our lives to His glory!

All of this and more is what is taking place the moment you repent of your sin and surrender your life to the lordship of Jesus. It is at this same time the Holy Spirit also baptizes you into the Body of Christ and you become a "living stone" in the Church (*see* 1 Peter 2:5).

# You Are God's 'Workmanship'

Without question, salvation — the first work of God's grace in your life — is beyond amazing! The apostle Paul made this point clear in Ephesians 2:10 where he said:

> **For we are his workmanship, created in Christ Jesus unto good works, which God hath before ordained that we should walk in them.**

Note the word "workmanship" — the marvelous Greek word *poiema*. It describes *a poem, a product, a literary masterpiece*, or *a shiny piece of art*. The fact that the Holy Spirit prompted Paul to select this word to describe the new, "saved" you means that when God birthed you into His family, He exerted all His creative power and ingenuity to make you into His masterpiece. And because you are His literary masterpiece, He is writing a brand-new story in your life — one that is filled with goodness, hope, and mercy (*see* Jeremiah 29:11).

Friend, you are "created in Christ Jesus unto good works" (Ephesians 2:10). The word "created" here is the Greek word *ktidzo*, which means *the creation of something from nothing*. This word tells us that rather than simply repair what was broken in you, the new "you" is a brand-spanking-new creative work of God! You are His shiny artwork — a living, breathing masterpiece of His mercy and grace.

All these wonderful things happened the moment you got saved, which is exactly what happened to Jesus' disciples when He breathed on them and said, "...Receive ye the Holy Ghost" (John 20:22).

# Salvation and the Baptism in the Spirit Are Two Separate Experiences

The indwelling of the Holy Spirit, which takes place at the moment of salvation, is not the same as the baptism in the Holy Spirit. The reason we know this to be true is because a few weeks *after* Jesus breathed on His disciples and told them to receive the Holy Spirit, He then told them:

> ...Behold, I send the promise of my Father upon you: but tarry ye in the city of Jerusalem, until ye be endued with power from on high.
>
> — Luke 24:49

Notice the first word "behold." It is the Greek word *idou*, which carries a sense of *amazement*. It was the equivalent of Jesus saying, *"Wow! Look at and listen to what I'm about to tell you!"* This word *idou* tells us Jesus was extremely excited about the promise of the Father that was coming in just a matter of days.

That promise was God's supernatural empowerment, which is signified by the word "endued." In Greek, the word "endued" is *enduo*, which means *to be empowered* or *to be clothed*. And the word "power" is the Greek word *dunamis*, which describes *explosive, superhuman power with enormous energy that produces phenomenal, extraordinary, and unparalleled results. Dunamis* is the very word used to denote *the force of an entire advancing army*, as well as the word for *a force of nature*, like *an earthquake, hurricane,* or *tornado*.

Through salvation, the disciples had received God's *peace*. But what they also needed was God's *power (dunamis)*, and that is what they were about to receive with the baptism in the Holy Spirit, the second work of grace.

## QUESTIONS AND ANSWERS WITH RICK RENNER

In the program, Rick answered the following question from one of our viewers.

**Q. What should I do if I become insensitive to the Lord?**

**A.** If you have been ignoring what the Lord has been prompting you to do, you have become insensitive to Him. To ignore His voice is to disobey Him, and when you disobey the Lord over and over again, it begins to numb your conscience, so you don't hear His voice like you did previously.

To make things right, you need to go to the Lord, repent for being disobedient, and ask the Holy Spirit to give you a *soft heart* that is sensitive to His touch (*see* Ezekiel 11:19,20; 36:25-27). It would also be good for you to spend time reading and meditating on scriptures in the book of Psalms, because it has a way of touching the heart and melting away the hardness, making it soft again.

Then the next time the Holy Spirit speaks to you, promptly obey Him. And keep feeding your spirit God's Word. It is the spiritual fuel that keeps the fire of your love and devotion burning red-hot for Him and helps you to be more sensitive to the voice of the Holy Spirit.

## STUDY QUESTIONS

Study to shew thyself approved unto God, a workman that
needeth not to be ashamed, rightly dividing the word of truth.
— 2 Timothy 2:15

1. The Bible records in John 20:19-22 that Jesus' disciples experienced salvation when He breathed on them in the Upper Room. Were you aware of this passage prior to this lesson? If so, what did you understand it to mean? How has your perspective changed?

2. When Jesus breathed on His disciples and said, "…Receive ye the Holy Ghost" (John 20:22), the Holy Spirit entered them and *never left*. What does John the Baptist say about Jesus in John 1:32 and 33 that is similar to what the disciples experienced?

3. Take a moment to carefully read through the *Renner Interpretive Version (RIV)* of Ephesians 1:14 in this lesson (p. 10). What is God showing you about the Holy Spirit being the "earnest" of your inheritance? How does Philippians 1:6 and Romans 8:29 and 30 relate to the meaning of Ephesians 1:14?

## PRACTICAL APPLICATION

But be ye doers of the word, and not hearers only,
deceiving your own selves.
— James 1:22

1. Can you remember the day you were born again? What was going on in your life at that time, and how did God make Himself real to you and reveal your need for salvation?

2. What new insights is the Holy Spirit showing you about being "sealed" by Him? When a package had a seal on it, what did it signify had already been done? What did it guarantee would happen to the package? How does this help you better understand the way God sees you?

## TOPIC
# The Second Work of Grace

## SCRIPTURES

1. **John 20:21,22** —Then said Jesus to them again, Peace be unto you: as my Father hath sent me, even so send I you. And when he had said this, he breathed on them, and saith unto them, Receive ye the Holy Ghost.

2. **Luke 24:49** — And, behold, I send the promise of my Father upon you: but tarry ye in the city of Jerusalem, until ye be endued with power from on high.

3. **Acts 1:4,5** — And, being assembled together with them, commanded them that they should not depart from Jerusalem, but wait for the promise of the Father, which, saith he, ye have heard of me. For John truly baptized with water; but ye shall be baptized with the Holy Ghost not many days hence.

4. **Acts 2:1-4** — And when the day of Pentecost was fully come, they were all with one accord in one place. And suddenly there came a sound from heaven as of a rushing mighty wind, and it filled all the house where they were sitting. And there appeared unto them cloven tongues like as of fire, and it sat upon each of them. And they were all filled with the Holy Ghost, and began to speak with other tongues, as the Spirit gave them utterance.

5. **Acts 8:12** — But when they believed Philip preaching the things concerning the kingdom of God, and the name of Jesus Christ, they were baptized, both men and women.

6. **Acts 8:14,15** — Now when the apostles which were at Jerusalem heard that Samaria had received the word of God, they sent unto them Peter and John: Who, when they were come down, prayed for them, that they might receive the Holy Ghost.

7. **Romans 8:9** — But ye are not in the flesh, but in the Spirit, if so be that the Spirit of God dwell in you. Now if any man have not the Spirit of Christ, he is none of his.

8. **Acts 8:21** — Thou hast neither part nor lot in this matter: for thy heart is not right in the sight of God.

9. **Acts 9:4,5** — And he fell to the earth, and heard a voice saying unto him, Saul, Saul, why persecutest thou me? And he said, Who art thou, Lord? And the Lord said, I am Jesus whom thou persecutest: it is hard for thee to kick against the pricks.

10. **Acts 9:17** — And Ananias went his way, and entered into the house; and putting his hands on him said, Brother Saul, the Lord, even Jesus, that appeared unto thee in the way as thou camest, hath sent me, that thou mightest receive thy sight, and be filled with the Holy Ghost.

11. **1 Corinthians 14:18** — I thank my God, I speak with tongues more than ye all.

12. **Acts 10:44,46** — While Peter yet spake these words, the Holy Ghost fell on all them which heard the word.... For they heard them speak with tongues, and magnify God....

13. **Acts 19:6** — And when Paul had laid his hands upon them, the Holy Ghost came on them; and they spake with tongues, and prophesied.

## GREEK WORDS

1. "behold" — ἰδοὺ (*idou*): wow; look; see; a sense of amazement

2. "endued" — ἐνδύω (*enduo*): to be empowered; to clothe

3. "power" — δύναμις (*dunamis*): explosive, superhuman power with enormous energy that produces phenomenal, extraordinary, and unparalleled results; the force of an entire army; a force of nature, like an earthquake, hurricane, or tornado

4. "matter" — λόγος (*logos*): words or speaking; you have neither part nor lot in this kind of speaking

## SYNOPSIS

In our first lesson, we learned about the first work of God's grace, which is *salvation*. For the disciples of Jesus, salvation took place the day He appeared to them in the Upper Room and breathed *into* them His Holy Spirit. The apostle John captured this event in his gospel, telling us:

> **Then said Jesus to them again, Peace be unto you: as my Father hath sent me, even so send I you. And when he had said this,**

he breathed on them, and saith unto them, Receive ye the Holy
Ghost.
— John 20:21,22

Again, we saw that the root of the word "breathed" in Greek literally
means *to breathe into* or *inflate*, just like one would breathe air into a balloon and fill it. And the word "receive," the Greek word *labete*, was Jesus'
command to His disciples *to take right now and actively receive* His Spirit.
That is what the disciples did, and instantly they were born again, making
them the first individuals in history to experience the new birth in Christ.

**The emphasis of this lesson:**

**The first work of God's grace is salvation, and the second work of grace
is the baptism in the Holy Spirit. The book of Acts gives us a clear, irrefutable pattern of people being saved and then subsequently being filled
with the Holy Spirit and speaking in tongues.**

# In Addition to God's Peace,
# We Also Need His *Power*

When people get saved, immediately they have *peace* with God. When
Jesus appeared to His disciples in the upper room and they experienced
salvation, He told them twice, "Peace be unto you" (John 20:19,21). *Peace*
is the fruit of salvation.

Sadly, while many Christians have experienced the peace of God, they live
powerless lives, and it is because they do not understand that there is a
second work of God's grace, which is called *the baptism in the Holy Spirit.*
*Peace* is the fruit of salvation, and *power* is the fruit of the baptism in the
Holy Spirit, which is why Jesus told His disciples to wait for the promise
of the Father to come upon them before trying to do anything for Him.
He said:

> **And, behold, I send the promise of my Father upon you: but
> tarry ye in the city of Jerusalem, until ye be endued with power
> from on high.**
> — Luke 24:49

To be clear, when Jesus spoke these words to His disciples in Luke 24:49,
they were already saved, so they had His peace. But that was not all they

needed. Jesus said, "There's more! You need the promise of My Father! You need to be endued with power from on high."

The word "endued" in Luke 24:49 is the Greek word *enduo*, which means *to be empowered*, and it depicts a person being *clothed*. Jesus was telling His friends, "You need to be clothed and fully dressed in God's power." That word "power" is a translation of the remarkable word *dunamis*, which describes *explosive, superhuman power with enormous energy that produces phenomenal, extraordinary, and unparalleled results*. It is the very word used to denote *the force of an entire advancing army*, as well as the word for *a force of nature*, like *an earthquake, hurricane,* or *tornado*.

This supernatural empowerment Jesus told His disciples to wait for would transform them into a spiritual force of nature that could really shake things up and blow away enemy opposition. It was so vital for them to be clothed in this power that Jesus' command to wait for it is found in Luke 24:49, which we just read, and in Acts 1:4 and 5, which says:

> **And, being assembled together with them, commanded them that they should not depart from Jerusalem, but wait for the promise of the Father, which, saith he, ye have heard of me. For John truly baptized with water; but ye shall be baptized with the Holy Ghost not many days hence.**

Again, the disciples were already saved when Jesus gave this command, which confirms that the baptism in the Holy Spirit was — and still is — a subsequent experience different from salvation.

# The Day of Pentecost Was Spiritual 'D-Day' for the Church

About ten days after Jesus instructed His disciples to wait in Jerusalem, the promise of the Father was released into His people. Luke documented what took place.

> **And when the day of Pentecost was fully come, they were all with one accord in one place. And suddenly there came a sound from heaven as of a rushing mighty wind, and it filled all the house where they were sitting. And there appeared unto them cloven tongues like as of fire, and it sat upon each of them. And**

they were all filled with the Holy Ghost, and began to speak
with other tongues, as the Spirit gave them utterance.

— Acts 2:1-4

This was unprecedented! For the first time ever in the history of mankind, the Holy Spirit of God came to the earth and took up permanent residence inside the very lives of people. This was the event prophesied by the prophet Joel more than 800 years earlier (*see* Joel 2:28,29). From the Day of Pentecost to the present, the baptism in the Holy Spirit continues to be the second work of grace God desires every believer to experience.

# Five Examples of the Baptism in the Holy Spirit

A careful study of the book of Acts reveals several examples of the second work of God's grace in the time of the Early Church.

### 1. The Believers Assembled in the Upper Room on the Day of Pentecost

The **first** people ever to be filled with the Holy Spirit were the 120 believers in the Upper Room who were praying and worshiping God on the Day of Pentecost. On that day, the world watched as individuals who had already received the first work of grace (salvation) received the second work of grace — the baptism in the Holy Spirit and began to speak in tongues.

### 2. Many Samaritans Experienced the Second Work of Grace

The **second** occurrence that took place is recorded in Acts 8. Philip, one of Jesus' original 12 apostles, had gone to Samaria and "preached Christ to them" (v. 5). Along with the preaching of the Good News, Philip did numerous miracles — the paralyzed and lame were healed, and those with unclean spirits were delivered.

Acts 8:12 says, "But when they believed Philip preaching the things concerning the kingdom of God, and the name of Jesus Christ, they were baptized, both men and women." To be clear, these people who "believed" what Philip preached were new believers who had just experienced the first work of grace. The baptism described here is water baptism. Thus, having repented of their sins and surrendering themselves to Jesus, the Holy Spirit had entered their hearts and placed God's seal of approval on them.

The Bible goes on to say, "Now when the apostles which were at Jerusalem heard that Samaria had received the word of God, they sent unto them Peter and John: Who, when they were come down, prayed for them, that they might receive the Holy Ghost" (Acts 8:14,15).

Some have mistakenly thought the phrase "that they might receive the Holy Ghost" is talking about these individuals getting saved, but what it's actually referring to is the *second* work of grace — the baptism in the Holy Spirit. We know from Acts 8:12 that they were already saved, and since they were already saved, the Holy Spirit was already living in them.

No one can be saved and not have the Holy Spirit. Romans 8:9 confirms this saying, "…Now if any man have not the Spirit of Christ, he is none of his." These Samaritans were saved (born again) and already had the Holy Spirit living inside them. What they needed was the second work of grace — the baptism in the Holy Spirit — which is what Peter and John prayed for them to receive. The Bible says:

> **(For as yet he** [the Spirit] **was fallen upon none of them: only they were baptized in the name of the Lord Jesus.)**
>
> **Then laid they their hands on them, and they received the Holy Ghost.**
>
> **— Acts 8:16,17**

At first glance, it may appear that these Samaritans didn't speak in tongues when they were baptized in the Spirit, but if you dig a bit deeper into the text, you'll see that they did. In verses 18 and 19, we see that a sorcerer named Simon offered Peter and John money so that he could have the ability to lay his hands on people and see them receive the Holy Spirit. Peter answered Simon by saying:

> **…Thy money perish with thee, because thou hast thought that the gift of God may be purchased with money. Thou hast neither part nor lot in this matter: for thy heart is not right in the sight of God.**
>
> **— Acts 8:20,21**

The word "matter" here is important. It is the Greek word *logos*, which means *words* or *speaking*. Hence, you could translate the first part of Acts 8:21, "You have neither part nor lot in these *words* or this *speaking*." The fact that this word *logos* — translated here as "matter" — is used, tells us that there was some unique type of speaking that resulted when Peter and John laid hands on the Samaritans. Indeed, they received the second work of God's grace and were baptized in the Holy Spirit and spoke in new tongues.

### 3. The Apostle Paul Was Baptized in the Holy Spirit

The pattern continued in the life of Saul, who later became known as the apostle Paul. Once Stephen was stoned for testifying that Jesus was — and is — the long-awaited Messiah, Saul began persecuting Christians in Jerusalem. After imprisoning some and scattering many others, Saul went to the Jewish leaders and received permission to begin persecuting Christians in other cities.

As he was en route to Damascus, he encountered the brilliant light of the presence of Jesus and was stopped dead in his tracks. The Bible says:

**And he fell to the earth, and heard a voice saying unto him, Saul, Saul, why persecutest thou me? And he said, Who art thou, Lord? And the Lord said, I am Jesus whom thou persecutest....**

**— Acts 9:4,5**

Notice that Saul called Jesus *Lord.* This is significant because Scripture says, "...No one can say that Jesus is Lord except by the Holy Spirit" (1 Corinthians 12:3 *NKJV*). The fact that Saul called Jesus *Lord* means that at that moment on the road to Damascus, he received the first work of grace. Saul was saved, and the Holy Spirit had taken up residence in his heart — sealing him with God's approval.

Three days later, while in the city of Damascus, Saul experienced the second work of grace through the ministry of a believer by the name of Ananias. The Bible says, "And Ananias went his way, and entered into the house; and putting his hands on him said, Brother Saul, the Lord, even Jesus, that appeared unto thee in the way as thou camest, hath sent me, that thou mightest receive thy sight, and be filled with the Holy Ghost. And immediately there fell from his eyes as it had been scales: and he received sight forthwith, and arose, and was baptized" (Acts 9:17,18).

So on the road to Damascus, Saul got saved, and while staying in the city in a house on Straight Street, Saul received the baptism in the Holy Spirit. These were two separate experiences — two different works of God's grace.

And if you are wondering if Saul — who became the apostle Paul — spoke in tongues, he most certainly did. In First Corinthians 14:18, he said:

**I thank my God, I speak with tongues more than ye all.**

This was Paul's own testimony that when he was baptized, he was filled with the Holy Spirit and spoke in new tongues.

### 4. Cornelius and His Family Were Baptized in the Holy Spirit

In the very next chapter of Acts, we are introduced to a Roman centurion named Cornelius. Unlike all the examples before him, Cornelius was not a Jew but a Gentile. What made him so unique in God's sight was that he was "a devout man, and one that feared God with all his house, which gave much alms to the people, and prayed to God always" (Acts 10:2).

Being directed by both a vision from God and the voice of the Holy Spirit, Peter journeyed to Caesarea where he met with Cornelius and his family and began to present the Gospel. But before Peter could complete his presentation, something extraordinary took place. The Bible says:

**While Peter yet spake these words, the Holy Ghost fell on all them which heard the word.**

**And they of the circumcision which believed were astonished, as many as came with Peter, because that on the Gentiles also was poured out the gift of the Holy Ghost.**

**For they heard them speak with tongues, and magnify God....**
**— Acts 10:44-46**

This event was unprecedented. Gentiles — for the first time ever — were baptized in the Holy Spirit and began speaking in new tongues. Apparently, Cornelius and his family received both the first and second works of grace *simultaneously*. Instead of happening on two separate occasions, they were saved and baptized in the Holy Spirit all at once.

### 5. Disciples of John the Baptist Were Baptized in the Holy Spirit

The next example of the baptism in the Holy Spirit is found in Acts 19, the events of which took place about 23 years *after* the Day of Pentecost. In this chapter, we find Paul entering the city of Ephesus where he encountered a group of disciples of John the Baptist. They had heard John preach and were baptized by him, but they had never heard of Jesus or the Holy Spirit (*see* Acts 19:1-3).

Immediately, Paul preached the Gospel to them; they were saved, and then he baptized them in the name of the Lord Jesus (*see* Acts 19:4,5). Although he could have said, "Great! You're saved. My job here is done," he didn't. He stayed with them and made sure they experienced the second work of grace too. The Bible says:

> **And when Paul had laid his hands upon them, the Holy Ghost came on them; and they spake with tongues, and prophesied.**
> **— Acts 19:6**

Once again, we see the repeated pattern: People experienced the first work of grace and were saved; they were then water baptized; and then they experienced the second work of grace where they were baptized in the Holy Spirit and began speaking in tongues. Essentially, this pattern is seen throughout the Early Church and is still seen today.

In all these examples, we find that there are two different works of grace, which are essential and fundamental to every believer's life: salvation, which is the new birth in Christ; and the baptism in the Holy Spirit, which is signified by speaking in tongues.

You may be asking, "Why tongues?" Great question! That will be the focus of our next lesson.

## QUESTIONS AND ANSWERS WITH RICK RENNER

In the program, Rick answered the following question from one of our viewers.

**Q. Why do people fall in God's presence?**

**A.** The first time that I saw someone fall when being prayed for, I was quite shocked. I had never seen that in my church when I was growing up. But I couldn't deny what I was seeing right in front of me. Sick people were lined up across the front of the church, and someone was laying hands on them and praying for them. Suddenly, the people being prayed for began falling to the ground. It literally looked like they were collapsing under the weight of something, which is exactly what was happening.

When the supernatural power of God came heavily upon these people, something had to give. Consequently, their knees weakened, and their feet slipped out from under them. Instantly, they collapsed onto the floor, which is exactly what happened to me in 1975 when I was a young man.

When I was prayed for, I collapsed onto the ground too. As I lay motionless on the floor, I felt the power of God radiating from my head to my feet, and back and forth. When I stood up again, I was miraculously healed. So if you've ever wondered why some people collapse in the presence of God, it's because the power of God has come upon them, and they cannot continue to stand under the weight of His mighty presence.

## STUDY QUESTIONS

**Study to shew thyself approved unto God, a workman that needeth not to be ashamed, rightly dividing the word of truth.**
**— 2 Timothy 2:15**

1. The command Jesus gave His disciples — to wait for the empowerment of the Holy Spirit — is a principle that we, too, must take to heart. Before we GO and try to do anything for God, we need to develop a healthy habit of waiting in His presence daily for fresh empowerment. What else does God promise you will happen when you take time to wait in His presence daily?
   - Isaiah 40:31
   - Psalm 25:4,5
   - Psalm 27:14
   - Psalm 62:1,2,5-7
   - Proverbs 20:22

2. The Day of Pentecost forever changed humanity. From that day forward, the Spirit of God came and began taking up permanent residence inside the very lives of His people. Take some time to meditate on these verses and ask the Holy Spirit to help you better understand the significance of Him living inside you.
   - 1 John 2:20 and 27
   - John 14:16,17 and 16:13-15

- Romans 8:9-11
- Romans 8:14-16

## PRACTICAL APPLICATION

But be ye doers of the word, and not hearers only,
deceiving your own selves.
—James 1:22

1. The word "power" — the Greek word *dunamis* — describes *explosive, superhuman power with enormous energy that produces phenomenal, extraordinary, and unparalleled results.* It is the very word used to denote *the force of an entire advancing army,* as well as the word for *a force of nature,* like *an earthquake, hurricane,* or *tornado.* Who do you know that exhibits this kind of spiritual power in their life? In what ways is it visible? What examples of this power can you see in *your* life?

2. After reading through the five examples of the baptism in the Holy Spirit documented in the book of Acts, which example (or examples) stood out to you most? Why? What do all these occurrences say to you personally about the importance of the baptism in the Holy Spirit in your own life?

## LESSON 3

## TOPIC

# Why Should You Speak in Tongues?

## SCRIPTURES

1. **Matthew 12:34** — …For out of the abundance of the heart the mouth speaketh.

2. **John 4:24** — God is a Spirit: and they that worship him must worship him in spirit and in truth.

3. **1 Corinthians 14:2,4** — For he that speaketh in an unknown tongue speaketh not unto men, but unto God: for no man understandeth him; howbeit in the spirit he speaketh mysteries…. He that speaketh in an

unknown tongue edifieth himself; but he that prophesieth edifieth the church.

4. **1 Corinthians 14:14-16** — For if I pray in an unknown tongue, my spirit prayeth, but my understanding is unfruitful. What is it then? I will pray with the spirit, and I will pray with the understanding also: I will sing with the spirit, and I will sing with the understanding also. Else when thou shalt bless with the spirit, how shall he that occupieth the room of the unlearned say Amen at thy giving of thanks, seeing he understandeth not what thou sayest?

5. **1 Corinthians 14:18** — I thank my God, I speak with tongues more than ye all.

## GREEK WORDS

No Greek words were shown in the program in this lesson.

## SYNOPSIS

In our last lesson, we saw that in the New Testament, there is a distinct pattern of God's interaction in people's lives. First, they were saved, which is the first work of grace, and then they had a subsequent experience called the baptism in the Holy Spirit, which is the second work of grace. We see this pattern from Acts 1 through Acts 19, which covers a span of about 23 years.

Once a person received the baptism in the Holy Spirit, they also spoke in tongues. This brings us to some very important questions, such as: What are tongues? Why is praying in tongues so important? What happens when a person prays in tongues? We'll answer these and other important questions in this third lesson.

**The emphasis of this lesson:**

**Praying in tongues is not "mere gibberish." It is a heavenly language given by God. When you receive the baptism in the Holy Spirit, the second work of grace, the tongue of your human spirit is loosed so you can communicate with God on the deepest level of intimacy possible.**

# Rick's Experience
## of Seeking the Baptism in the Holy Spirit

It is often very helpful to hear what others experienced in their personal walk with God, which is why Rick took the time to share what he went through as he diligently sought to receive the baptism in the Holy Spirit. Here's what he said.

When I was a young man, I became really hungry for the things of God, and I began to seek the baptism in the Holy Spirit. At that time, I didn't realize how easy it was to receive this second work of grace. Nevertheless, I prayed and prayed to be baptized in the Spirit, constantly seeking the Lord for this gift. Finally, the day came when I opened my heart, and I was gloriously baptized in the Holy Spirit.

I had been saved much earlier in my life, so I already had peace with God. I knew that if I died, I was going to Heaven. The problem was I didn't have any power. In fact, our church was basically powerless. Although we went out regularly to share the Gospel and testify of God's goodness, we were all scared to do it. The truth is, I was terrified to go out and witness because I was trying to do it in my own strength.

*Power* comes with the second work of grace, which is the baptism in the Holy Spirit. When I did finally receive the Spirit's baptism, the power of God hit me, and I knew I had been filled — no question about it. What was puzzling to me was that I did not immediately speak in tongues. That didn't happen until several hours later.

Looking back, I believe this was because someone was with me when I received the Spirit's baptism, and I was a little timid about speaking in tongues in front of them. When I finally got into a place where I was by myself, I got on my knees and said, "Alright Lord. I've been filled with the Spirit, now I want my spirit to pray in tongues."

I then began to pray in English, and suddenly new words began to come out of my mouth. Then a thought came to me, *What are you doing? You're just making that up. It's not real.* So, I stopped. But then I heard the Holy Spirit say, "No, no. What you're doing is right. Keep going."

So I started praying in tongues again. But the same fearful thought that I was making it up returned, so I stopped again. Then once more, I heard the Holy Spirit say, "Come on! One more time. Just let it go." So I began speaking in tongues again, and this time — BAM! It was like a river began to flow out of my inner man. And that is what happens when you get filled with the Holy Spirit.

## Your Mouth Is the Outlet for What's in You

In Matthew 12:34, Jesus said, "…Out of the abundance of the heart the mouth speaketh." Whatever your heart is filled with is going to come out of your mouth. If your heart is filled with unforgiveness, words of unforgiveness are going to come out of your mouth. Likewise, if your heart is filled with anxiety and fear, words of anxiety and fear are going to come out of your mouth.

Your mouth is the outlet for what is in you. That is what Jesus meant when He said, "…Out of the abundance of the heart the mouth speaketh" (Matthew 12:34). If you are filled with joy and peace, words of joy and peace will be released from your lips. Again, your mouth is the outlet for what is in you.

When we apply this principle to the book of Acts, we see that every time people's hearts were filled with the Holy Spirit, tongues came out of their mouths. This is an irrefutable pattern from Acts 2 through Acts 19. The very first example is, of course, when the 120 followers of Christ were in the Upper Room in Jerusalem on the Day of Pentecost. The Word says, "And they were all filled with the Holy Ghost, and began to speak with other tongues, as the Spirit gave them utterance" (Acts 2:4).

Notice that it says, "…The Spirit gave them utterance" (Acts 2:4). They were filled with the Spirit, so words of the Spirit came out of their mouths. That is what happens when anyone experiences this second work of God's grace. When a person is baptized in the Holy Spirit, the tongue of his spirit is loosed, and he begins to speak from his spirit in a heavenly language we call tongues.

Tongues are not "mere gibberish"; they are your human spirit speaking to God by His Spirit — by the agency of the Holy Spirit. Tongues are spiritual words flowing up from your heart and out of your mouth. Speaking in tongues is a very real, legitimate prayer language.

## Your Human Spirit Is the 'Real You'

Each one of us is a three-part being. We are a spirit, we have a soul, and we live in a physical body. The apostle Paul makes this clear in First Thessalonians 5:23. Although most people are aware of and focus on the body because it is the part of us we can see, the soul and spirit are also very real and very important.

Beneath the shell of the body lies the soul, which is the *mind*, the *will*, and the *emotions*. Beneath the soul, is the human spirit, which is *the real you*. It is the deepest part of you that was totally transformed into the likeness of Jesus the moment you got saved (*see* 2 Corinthians 5:17). It is also that place where the Holy Spirit comes to live.

Your spirit is the very core of your being. It lives in your body, thinks and makes decisions through your soul, and longs to communicate with the Spirit of God. The deepest, most intimate level of communication you can have with God is spirit to spirit, which is exactly what the baptism in the Holy Spirit makes possible.

## Spirit Speaks *Spirit*

Think for a moment. What do Germans speak? That's right — they speak *German*. What do Italians speak? Right again — they speak *Italian*. How about French people and Spanish people? That's right — the French speak *French*, and the Spanish speak *Spanish*.

So what language do you think a *spirit* speaks? If you said *spirit*, you are correct! The language of the human spirit is *spirit*, which really helps us better understand what Jesus said in John 4:24:

> **God is a Spirit: and they that worship him must worship him in spirit and in truth.**

Did you catch that? God is a Spirit, and the deepest part of you is spirit. Therefore, to talk to God most effectively, we must communicate with our spirit to His Spirit. That is what the baptism in the Holy Spirit makes possible! The Holy Spirit in you, looses the tongue of your spirit, and enabling you to speak (pray) in a spiritual, heavenly language. When you pray in the Spirit (or in tongues), you bypass the limitations of your mind and speak directly to the heart of God.

When we just pray in English (or our native language), eventually we run out of words to say. Rick's wife, Denise, experienced this firsthand before she was baptized in the Holy Spirit. As she was lying in bed one night trying to worship the Lord, she ran out of words to express her love to Jesus. Frustrated, she said, "Lord, I've run out of words. I need the baptism in the Holy Spirit and the heavenly prayer language that comes with it to communicate my love more fully to You."

Sure enough, when she asked God for the baptism in the Spirit, she received it. Suddenly, the tongue of her spirit was loosed, and she moved into a realm of prayer like she had never experienced in her entire life. That is what the spiritual language of tongues provides — it exceeds human vocabulary, enabling your spirit to speak directly to God who is also a Spirit. It is the highest level of prayer and intercession you can experience.

Again, speaking in tongues is not "mere gibberish"; it is truly the language of the human spirit crying out to God in the purest language possible. Does this mean you should no longer pray in your own native language? No. Praying in the language you understand is helpful because it develops your mind and helps you to know the will of God. According to Scripture, you are to pray with your mind *and* your spirit — using both your native tongue and the gift of heavenly tongues that the Holy Spirit provides (*see* 1 Corinthians 14:14,15).

## God's Spirit Has All the Answers, and His Spirit Is Living in You

When you pray in tongues, some extraordinary things take place. The apostle Paul talks about these benefits in his first letter to the believers at Corinth. First, he said:

**For he that speaketh in an unknown tongue speaketh not unto men, but unto God: for no man understandeth him; howbeit in the spirit he speaketh mysteries.**
— **1 Corinthians 14:2**

Notice the word "speaketh," used three times in this verse. It is a translation of the Greek word *laleo*, which means *to talk, to speak*, or *to converse*. It carries the idea of using words in order to declare one's mind and disclose one's thoughts. Its repeated use establishes the fact that tongues are a real language.

Now if you have a *King James Version*, you'll see that the word "unknown" is italicized, which means it was added by the translators; it's not in the original text. The purpose of adding the word "unknown" is to show that this "tongue" is a language that is not naturally known to you. It is a spiritual language. When we insert the meaning of the word "speaketh," we could translate First Corinthians 14:2 to say:

**For he that *talks* or *converses* in an unknown tongue *talks* and *converses* not to men, but to God: for no man understandeth him; howbeit in the Spirit, he *speaks* and *declares* mysteries.**

This brings us to the word "mysteries," which is the Greek word *musterion*, and it describes *something hidden, a secret*, or *a mystery*. It includes *the secret counsels, purpose, and will of God*. Interestingly, one of the number-one prayer requests of believers is to know the will of God for their life, which often is a mystery to them as they journey through life. But it doesn't have to be.

As we learned in a previous lesson, the moment you are saved, the Holy Spirit enters your life and takes up permanent residence inside your heart. In addition to placing His tamper-proof, spiritual seal on you, He brings the fullness of God into your life in divine "Seed" form (*see* 1 John 3:9). Thus, the Holy Spirit brings the mind of God, which includes the will of God for your life, when He moves into you. In other words, He has every answer to every question you will ever ask because the Holy Spirit knows it all!

Friend, the answers you need are not floating somewhere in the atmosphere. They are *in* you because the Holy Spirit is in you. First Corinthians 14:2 tells us that when you begin to pray in tongues, you literally begin to release those mysteries from deep within your spirit. As you pray in tongues, you begin to dredge your human spirit, and the Spirit of God begins to bring all the answers up to your mind, giving you the understanding you need to know.

## Praying in Tongues
## Expands Your Spiritual Capacity

What else happens when you pray in tongues? The apostle Paul continued:

**He that speaketh in an unknown tongue edifieth himself; but he that prophesieth edifieth the church.**
— **1 Corinthians 14:4**

Once more, we see the word "speaketh"— the Greek word *laleo* — which means *to talk, to speak,* or *to converse.* As in verse 2, the use of this word tells us clearly that the "tongue" being described is a real language in which one converses. Here, Paul said that anyone who speaks in a tongue "edifieth" himself.

In Greek, the word "edifieth" is the remarkable Greek word *oikodome*, which is an architectural term that was used to describe *the expansion of a building.* If you had a house that could no longer accommodate everything and everyone, you would need to expand it by pushing out the walls and raising the roof to make more room.

In First Corinthians 14:4, Paul used this word *oikodome* (edifieth) to describe what happens in the spirit realm when we pray in tongues. Spiritually speaking, praying in the language of the Spirit pushes out our walls and raises the roof, giving us greater ability to accommodate more of the Holy Spirit in our life. Essentially, praying in tongues expands our spiritual capacity.

For example, let's say you are reading a scripture in the Bible, and you don't understand what it means. Or maybe you're walking through challenges, and you really need the wisdom of God to help you make the right decisions. These are both perfect opportunities to begin praying in tongues so that your spiritual capacity can be expanded to receive the divine revelation you need from the Holy Spirit.

# For the Best Results,
## Pray in the Spirit *and* Pray With Your Mind

The apostle Paul added more clarification to what happens when we pray in the language of the spirit in First Corinthians 14:14. Here, he said:

> **For if I pray in an unknown tongue, my spirit prayeth, but my understanding is unfruitful.**

In this verse, Paul mentioned the word "pray" twice, which refers to your human spirit speaking and conversing with God. He said that when you pray in tongues, it is your spirit praying, but your understanding (your mind) is unfruitful — your mind doesn't understand it. To deal with this dilemma, Paul added:

> **What is it then? I will pray with the spirit, and I will pray with the understanding also: I will sing with the spirit, and I will sing with the understanding also.**
> **— 1 Corinthians 14:15**

Here, Paul brought a healthy balance to our prayer life, by telling us that we should pray "with the spirit" (or in tongues) and pray "with the understanding," which means with words our mind comprehends. Both have great value. In fact, they are so valuable that Paul said we are also to sing "in the Spirit" (in tongues) *and* sing "with the understanding," which again refers to words our mind comprehends.

Interestingly, Paul then said, "Else when thou shalt *bless* with the spirit…" (1 Corinthians 14:16). This lets us know that when we are praying in tongues, we are also *blessing* God. We are thanking Him and praising Him with the highest level of worship we can offer, and it is through speaking in tongues.

Are you beginning to see the importance of praying in tongues? It is vital in the life of every believer. It's one of the reasons Paul said, "I thank my God, I speak with tongues more than ye all" (1 Corinthians 14:18).

Remember, Paul wrote nearly two-thirds of the New Testament, which was more than any other person. It was by praying in tongues that he expanded his spiritual capacity and increased his ability to receive more and more revelation and divine insight from the Holy Spirit. Friend, if the apostle Paul needed to speak in tongues, we need to speak in tongues too.

# QUESTIONS AND ANSWERS WITH RICK RENNER

In the program, Rick answered the following question from one of our viewers.

**Q. Is speaking in tongues praying in a real foreign language?**

**A.** In general, speaking in tongues is the language of your own human spirit as it converses with God. This is very clearly explained in First Corinthians 14:14-16.

However, there are moments when you may give a message in tongues that somebody understands in his or her own native language. One day when I was on a beach sharing the message of Christ with some people, I became flustered and frustrated and didn't know what else to say. In that difficult moment, I began to pray in tongues, and suddenly, the people to whom I was witnessing understood me because I was speaking in their native language.

While that does happen at times, usually when we pray in tongues, it is the voice of our own human spirit communicating with God in a heavenly language — a language which we can also use to sing to the Lord.

# STUDY QUESTIONS

**Study to shew thyself approved unto God, a workman that needeth not to be ashamed, rightly dividing the word of truth.**
**— 2 Timothy 2:15**

1. Using the Bible itself, what are the purposes for — and blessings that come with — praying in tongues? Which of these have you personally experienced?
   • **1 Corinthians 14:2**: _____

   _____

   • **1 Corinthians 14:4** (and in Jude 1:20): _____

   _____

   • **1 Corinthians 14:14,16**: _____

   _____

   • **1 Corinthians 14:22** (Acts 2:5-12 is an example): _____

   _____

2. The apostle Paul said, "I thank my God I speak with tongues more than you all; yet *in the church* I would rather speak five words with my understanding, that I may teach others also, than ten thousand words in a tongue" (1 Corinthians 14:18,19 *NKJV*). So while speaking in tongues in a church setting is good, there are guidelines.

 - According to **First Corinthians 14:27 and 28**, what are the guidelines for speaking in tongues in a church setting?

 - According to **First Corinthians 14:26**, what is the primary and ultimate purpose for tongues and everything else done in the church?

 - According to **First Corinthians 14:40**, how should all things be done?

## PRACTICAL APPLICATION

But be ye doers of the word, and not hearers only,
deceiving your own selves.
—James 1:22

1. Coming into this lesson on tongues, you probably had some questions on the subject. What answers did you receive? How has the teaching helped you better understand the purpose of tongues? What is your greatest takeaway?

2. Have you been baptized in the Holy Spirit and received the gift of tongues? If so, how would describe your experience? How has this deeper level of intimacy with the Spirit changed your life? How would you encourage a friend to seek the baptism in the Holy Spirit?

3. If you have not been baptized in the Holy Spirit but would like to be, you can! All you have to do is ask — that's what Jesus Himself says about the Holy Spirit in Luke 11:9-13. Take time to read this passage and get alone with God. If you have any unconfessed sin your life, simply repent and ask Jesus to baptize you in the Holy Spirit.

## Prayer To Be Filled With the Holy Spirit

*Lord, You gave the Holy Spirit to Your Church to help us fulfill the Great Commission. I ask You in faith for this free gift, and I receive right now the baptism in the Holy Spirit. I believe You hear me as I pray, and I thank You for baptizing me in the Holy Spirit with the evidence of speaking with a new, supernatural prayer language. In Jesus' name. Amen.*

TOPIC

# The By-Product of the Baptism in the Holy Spirit

## SCRIPTURES

1. **John 20:20-22** — And when he had so said, he shewed unto them his hands and his side. Then were the disciples glad, when they saw the Lord. Then said Jesus to them again, Peace be unto you: as my Father hath sent me, even so send I you. And when he had said this, he breathed on them, and saith unto them, Receive ye the Holy Ghost.

2. **Luke 24:49** — And, behold, I send the promise of my Father upon you: but tarry ye in the city of Jerusalem, until ye be endued with power from on high.

3. **Acts 1:4,5** — And, being assembled together with them, commanded them that they should not depart from Jerusalem, but wait for the promise of the Father, which, saith he, ye have heard of me. For John truly baptized with water; but ye shall be baptized with the Holy Ghost not many days hence.

4. **Acts 1:8** — But ye shall receive power, after that the Holy Ghost is come upon you: and ye shall be witnesses unto me both in Jerusalem, and in all Judaea, and in Samaria, and unto the uttermost part of the earth.

5. **Ephesians 6:10** — Finally, my brethren, be strong in the Lord, and in the power of his might.

## GREEK WORDS

1. "behold" — ἰδού (*idou*): wow; look; see; a sense of amazement
2. "endued" — ἐνδύω (*enduo*): to be empowered; to clothe

3. "power" — δύναμις (*dunamis*): explosive, superhuman power with enormous energy that produces phenomenal, extraordinary, and unparalleled results; the force of an entire army; a force of nature, like an earthquake, hurricane, or tornado

4. "receive" — Λάβετε (*labete*): to take right now; to actively receive

5. "strong" — ἐνδύω (*enduo*): to be empowered; to clothe

## SYNOPSIS

You are a spirit — that's the real you, and it's natural for a spirit to speak. When your spirit begins to speak, it speaks a *spiritual* language, and this is made possible through the baptism in the Holy Spirit. When you receive the Spirit's baptism, the tongue of your spirit is loosed and you are enabled to speak in a way you have never spoken before.

The Bible calls this language *tongues*, and it is the highest means by which you can pray, most supernatural kind of prayer. In praying in tongues, your spirit bypasses your mind and communicates directly with God, spirit to Spirit. And this experience is for everyone. Acts 2:39 says, "For the promise is unto you, and to your children, and to all that are afar off, even as many as the Lord our God shall call."

If you've not received the baptism in the Holy Spirit, that does not make you a second-class Christian. It just means there's more that God wants you to receive. You've already received the peace of God through salvation, but what you also need is the power of God. And that power comes from the second work of grace — the baptism in the Holy Spirit!

**The emphasis of this lesson:**

**The result of getting baptized in the Holy Spirit is an enduement of supernatural power. God wants you to settle and get comfortable in His power, allowing it to flow in and through your life. Clothed in the Spirit's power, you can defeat the devil's attacks and overcome life's problems.**

## The Disciples Were Saved and Sealed in the Holy Spirit

For three and a half years, the disciples walked with Jesus — watching, listening, and learning from all that He did. But after Jesus was arrested, brutally beaten, and crucified, the 11 took to hiding in an upper room in the city of Jerusalem. Three days later, while huddled together in seclusion, Jesus appeared to them behind closed doors, giving them proof that He had indeed been raised from the dead.

John 20:20-22 documents this event:

**And when he had so said, he shewed unto them his hands and his side. Then were the disciples glad, when they saw the Lord.**

**Then said Jesus to them again, Peace be unto you: as my Father hath sent me, even so send I you.**

**And when he had said this, he breathed on them, and saith unto them, Receive ye the Holy Ghost.**

Up until that moment, the disciples were like every other follower of God in the Old Testament. During that time, the Holy Spirit did not live inside anyone's human spirit. Instead, the Spirit of God would temporarily come upon individuals, empower them for certain assignments, and then leave them. Although the Spirit did return to empower people for another task, He did not permanently live inside them.

The day Jesus *breathed* on the disciples, all that changed.

As we noted, the word "breathed" in Greek is *emphusao*, which literally means *to breathe into* or *inflate*. It would be just like putting a balloon to your lips, blowing into it, and watching it expand as it received your breath. In the same way, Jesus breathed into them, and they received the Holy Spirit.

The word "receive" is the Greek word *labete*, the direct form of the word *lambano*, which means *to take right now* and *to actively receive*. That's what the disciples did. They took into themselves His Spirit, and instantly they were born again, making them the first individuals in history to experience the new birth in Christ.

What the disciples experienced in John 20 was *salvation* — the first work of God's grace. In that moment, they not only received the Holy Spirit, but they were also *sealed* in the Holy Spirit. For the first time, they had the peace of God.

That is what happens when you surrender your life to Jesus. You receive God's peace. Suddenly, you're no longer worried about your eternal destiny because you know that you know that you're saved. You have the peace of God, and you're at peace with God because the Prince of Peace has taken up residence in your life.

## Jesus Was *Excited* To Share the News of the Holy Spirit's Coming!

But peace wasn't the only thing Jesus wanted His disciples to have. He knew they needed to experience the second work of grace, which is the baptism in the Holy Spirit. It is distinctly different from salvation and usually takes place *after* a person gets saved.

Just before ascending back into Heaven to take His rightful place at the right hand of the Father, Jesus told His disciples, "And, behold, I send the promise of my Father upon you: but tarry ye in the city of Jerusalem, until ye be endued with power from on high" (Luke 24:49).

Jesus was so excited about the news He was sharing that He began His message with the word "behold," which in Greek is the word *idou*. Essentially, it means *wow*, and it carries a sense of *amazement*. The use of this word tells us that Jesus was injecting His own sense of excitement into what He was about to say. He was so thrilled about what His disciples were going to receive in just a few days that He basically said, "Wow! This is amazing! Guys, listen to this!"

He then added, "…I send the promise of my Father upon you…" (Luke 24:49). That promise is the baptism in the Holy Spirit. Since Jesus had already breathed the Holy Spirit into His disciples a few weeks earlier and they were saved and sealed with the Spirit, this promise of the Spirit coming "upon" them had to be something different — something additional.

## Get Comfortable and Settle Into the 'Power' of the Holy Spirit

Jesus continued by commanding His disciples, "…But tarry ye in the city of Jerusalem, until ye be endued with power from on high" (Luke 24:49). We saw that the word "endued" is the Greek word *enduo*, which is very important. It means *to be empowered* or *to be clothed*, and it carries the idea of a person that is so comfortable in his apparel that he settles down into his new set of clothes and feels at home.

What's fascinating is that the "clothing" Jesus is referring to here is "power," and the Greek word for "power" is the marvelous word *dunamis.* This is the old Greek word that described *explosive, superhuman power with enormous energy that produces phenomenal, extraordinary, and unparalleled results.* Dunamis is the very word used by both the Greeks and the Romans to describe *the full might of the advancing Roman army* as well as *a force of nature* like *an earthquake, a hurricane,* or *a tornado.*

By using the word *dunamis,* Jesus is saying that when you're clothed with the power of the Holy Spirit, His power will turn you into *a supernatural force of nature* in the realm of the spirit!

- Like a hurricane, you'll be able to *blow evil out of the way.*

- Like an earthquake, you'll be able to *shake things up.*

- Like a tornado, you'll be able to *annihilate things* that need to be removed.

Likewise, by using the word *dunamis,* Jesus is saying the Holy Spirit's power in your life will transform you into *a single-man army,* enabling you to advance His Kingdom and to demonstrate unparalleled, extraordinary supernatural power. That's how much power is going to be in you and working through you.

Again, because Jesus used the word "endued" — which depicts *settling into a set of clothes* — it means that when you receive the second work of grace, which is the baptism in the Holy Spirit, He wants you to get comfortable and settle into His power. Just like settling into an old set of clothes in which you feel at ease, you are to operate in power and be comfortable in power. Remember, power is the byproduct of receiving this divine endue-ment.

# You Need the Spirit's Power
# To Defeat the Devil's Attacks and Overcome Problems

Church history tells us that both the gospel of Luke and the book of Acts were written by Luke. Interestingly, God moved on Luke's heart to end his gospel and begin the book of Acts with the same instructions Jesus gave His disciples just before ascending into Heaven. In Acts 1:4 and 5, he said:

> **And, being assembled together with them, commanded them that they should not depart from Jerusalem, but wait for the promise of the Father, which, saith he, ye have heard of me. For John truly baptized with water; but ye shall be baptized with the Holy Ghost not many days hence.**

Keep in mind that when Jesus gave this command to His disciples, it was a few weeks after He had breathed on them to receive the Holy Spirit, so they were already saved and sealed with the Holy Spirit. Through salvation, they had the peace of God, but that was not enough. They still needed the power of God. Jesus knew the devil is real and that they would come up against many problems in the world. It was the baptism in the Holy Spirit that would give them the supernatural strength they needed to carry out the Great Commission.

Rick shared how when he grew up, the church he attended didn't believe in the secondary work of grace. Like many other Christians, he was taught that the baptism in the Holy Spirit and the gifts of the Spirit ended with the death of the apostles. Sadly, what they believed was exactly what they received. Since they didn't believe in power, they never experienced power. They were peaceful, powerless people.

Thankfully, Jesus didn't just give us peace — He also gave us the *dunamis* power of His Spirit! It is the supernatural strength we need to deal with the enemy and the problems we face. It is the divine anointing that enables us to heal the sick and cast out devils. Friend, you need the Holy Spirit's power because there are many things in life that must be overcome. He is the Greater One who lives in you, and He is greater than the enemy in this world (*see* 1 John 4:4).

## You Shall 'Receive Power'!

Along with His command to wait in Jerusalem, Jesus said, "But ye shall receive power, after that the Holy Ghost is come upon you: and ye shall be witnesses unto me both in Jerusalem, and in all Judaea, and in Samaria, and unto the uttermost part of the earth" (Acts 1:8).

Again, we see the word "power" — the Greek word *dunamis*. What this means is that when the power of God comes upon you through the baptism in the Holy Spirit, the Spirit clothes you with extraordinary, unparalleled power. It transforms you into a one-man army with the ability to advance like you were never able to advance before.

Likewise, it turns you into a spiritual force of nature to shake things up and blow the enemy out of the way. That's what the word power — *dunamis* — means and what Jesus said you will receive after the Holy Spirit comes upon you.

This brings us to the word "receive," which happens to be the very same word used in Luke 24:49 — the Greek word *labete*, a direct form of the word *lambano*, meaning *to receive* as well as *to take*. The idea you need to understand here is that Jesus wants to give you this power, but you also have to *receive it* or *take it* by faith. In other words, it requires your cooperation just like salvation.

For you to get saved, you must cooperate by acknowledging you are a sinner and asking Jesus to forgive you, cleanse you, and be the Lord of your life. If you don't repent and ask the Lord to save you, you are not saved.

In the same way, Jesus wants to give you this secondary work of grace — the baptism in the Holy Spirit. He is ready to baptize you right now, but you must take it. You have to receive it by faith. All you need to do is simply say, "Jesus, baptize me in the Holy Spirit," and — *bam!* — He will flood you with divine power. You'll speak in tongues, and new power will begin to operate in and through your life.

# Be 'Strong in the Lord'

When you study the book of Acts, you'll see that something extraordinary occurred after the disciples were clothed in the Spirit's power. These men, who were once fearful and hiding behind locked doors, were now set ablaze with the fire of the Holy Spirit, and suddenly, they emerged onto the streets, boldly preaching and declaring the Good News about Jesus. In His name, they began healing the sick and casting out demons.

As a matter of fact, Acts 5 tells us that there were so many people needing to be healed that Peter laid hands on people who were lined up on one side of the street while his shadow passed over sick people on the other side of the street. Both groups of people were healed — those he touched with his hands as well as the ones his shadow touched. That's how much power was manifesting.

You might say Peter was "…strong in the Lord, and in the power of his might." That is exactly what the Bible tells us in Ephesians 6:10. Just before he described all the spiritual weapons of our warfare, the apostle Paul began the wrap-up of his letter to the Ephesian believers by saying:

**Finally, my brethren, be strong in the Lord, and in the power of his might.**

In this verse, the word "strong" is the Greek word *enduo*, the same word translated "endued" in Luke 24:49. Something additional to note about this word is that it's a compound of the word *en* and the word *duo*. The word *en* means to be *in* something — like to be *in* a vase, *in* a vessel, or *in* some kind of a receptacle.

The second word *duo* is derived from the Greek word *dunamis*, which describes *the supernatural, extraordinary power of the Spirit*. When these two words are compounded to form *enduo*, it means *to be clothed with power* or to take this divine supernatural power and place it *in* something. This tells us that *dunamis* power was not created to be free floating in the atmosphere. Instead, it was designed to be placed into some kind of vessel or receptacle.

That's where *we* come in. We are divinely fashioned by God to be the receptacle for this power. God wants to fill us and clothe us with this divine power, and when we cooperate with Him and allow Him to fill and clothe us, something extraordinary happens.

## Be Strong in the 'Power' of His Might

Taking another look at Paul's words in Ephesians 6:10, we read, "…Be strong in the Lord, and in the power of his might."

The word "power" here is not *dunamis*, but instead, the Greek word *kratos*, and it describes the *eruptive* or *demonstrated power of God*. This is not theoretical power that one intellectually believes in — it is raw force and strength that is visible for all to see. It's an undeniable power you can see, feel, and experience.

For example, if you had been one of the soldiers at the tomb on the morning of the resurrection, you would have been an eyewitness to *kratos* power. God shook the earth with a mighty quake, rolled back the massive gravestone, and brought the dead body of Jesus back to life!

This wasn't power they just "heard" about — it was power they visibly experienced and personally felt. It is power that would be classified as signs, wonders, and supernatural feats.

## What's the Difference Between 'Power' and 'Might'?

When you read, "…Be strong in the Lord, and in the power of his might" (Ephesians 6:10), you may think the words *power* and *might* are the same, but they're not. We've seen that the Greek word for "power" here is *kratos*, which is the *demonstrated, eruptive power of God*. The word "might" is different. It is the Greek word *ischus*, and it describes *a man that is bound with muscles*. We would call him a bodybuilder, having huge, strapping muscles that are bulging everywhere. He's a mighty man and able to do mighty things.

The One being described in Ephesians 6:10 who has *might* is the Lord. This means when you receive the baptism in the Holy Spirit and are clothed (*enduo*) with His divine power, in some indescribable way, you become connected to the mighty, muscular ability of God. That's the power of his might.

You may be thinking, *What kind of muscles does God have?* Well, if we could see Him in the realm of the spirit, we would say He is Mr. Universe, in the truest sense of the word. No one has greater muscular ability than God! And somehow, when we receive the infilling of the Holy Spirit, we become divinely connected to God's mighty muscular abilities.

The way we activate His spiritual might is by praying in the Spirit, praying God's Word in the name of Jesus, and obediently doing what He instructs us to do. With that, God flexes His muscles and divine *kratos* power flows through us to perform signs, wonders, and mighty deeds that are extraordinary, unparalleled, *dunamis* power.

Friend, when you receive the second work of grace, which is the baptism in the Holy Spirit, it is natural for you to begin moving in divine power, because divine power is the byproduct of the baptism in the Holy Spirit.

## QUESTIONS AND ANSWERS WITH RICK RENNER

In the program, Rick answered the following question from one of our viewers.

**Q. I've been praying for the baptism in the Holy Spirit for many years, but I've never spoken in tongues. What should I do?**

**A.** Praying in tongues is a promised gift that belongs to any person who has been baptized in the Holy Spirit. In fact, if you study the entire book of Acts, you'll see that every time someone was baptized in the Spirit, it was always accompanied by them speaking in tongues.

To be clear, speaking in tongues is just the release of your human spirit, which then begins to fellowship in a spiritual language with God. The Bible tells us in First Corinthians 14:2 that when you pray in tongues, you speak to God, and you speak divine mysteries or secrets. Speaking in the spiritual language of tongues is one of the highest levels of prayer that exists.

If you want someone to pray with you to receive the baptism in the Holy Spirit with the ability to pray in tongues, reach out to us right now by calling 1-800-742-5593. Our team will join our faith with your faith and believe for the promised gift of the Holy Spirit's infilling for your life, just as it has been given to countless others since the birth of the Church on the Day of Pentecost.

## STUDY QUESTIONS

*Study to shew thyself approved unto God, a workman that needeth not to be ashamed, rightly dividing the word of truth.*
— 2 Timothy 2:15

1.  When you surrender your life to Jesus, you receive God's *peace*. Your eternal destiny is secure, and in every moment, you can have the calm assurance of knowing that the same mighty God Who holds all things together is FOR you (*see* Romans 8:31). Take some time to read and meditate on what the Bible says about the power and importance of God's peace.

    • John 14:27

    • Colossians 3:15

    • Philippians 4:6,7

    • Psalm 4:8

    • John 16:33

2. The Bible says, "For though we walk (live) in the flesh, we are not carrying on our warfare according to the flesh and using mere human weapons. For the weapons of our warfare are not physical [weapons of flesh and blood], but they are mighty before God for the overthrow and destruction of strongholds" (2 Corinthians 10:3,4 *AMPC*). Read these passages that identify the spiritual weapons God has given you to fight against the enemy:

   • **The Blood:** Revelation 12:11; Hebrews 9:11-14; 1 Peter 1:18,19; 1 John 1:7

   • **The Name:** Philippians 2:9-11; John 14:13,14; 15:16; Acts 3:6,16; 16:18

   • **The Word:** Hebrews 4:12; Jeremiah 23:29; Romans 1:16; Ephesians 6:14,17; James 1:21

   • **The Armor:** Ephesians 6:13-18

## PRACTICAL APPLICATION

*But be ye doers of the word, and not hearers only,*
*deceiving your own selves.*
*— James 1:22*

1. Rick shared how in his youth, the church he attended didn't believe in the secondary work of grace. Like many other Christians, he was taught that the baptism in the Holy Spirit and the gifts of the Spirit ended with the death of the apostles. What were you taught about the baptism in the Holy Spirit? Do you feel any differently now that you've gone through this lesson? If so, what stands out to you as a new truth you weren't taught before?

2. When Jesus told His disciples to wait for the empowerment of the Spirit, He said that they would be "endued" with power. The meaning of this word depicts *becoming comfortable and settling into a set of clothes,* which is what God wants you to do with His power. Are you comfortable and do you feel at home in the power of God working in and through your life? What is one thing about His power and might that you want to become more comfortable with experiencing?

3. Have you ever seen God's visible, *kratos* power at work in someone else? If so, describe what you witnessed firsthand. What do you most remember or want to see replicated in your life?

TOPIC

# Other Benefits of Being Filled With the Holy Spirit

## SCRIPTURES

1.  **Ephesians 5:17,18** — Wherefore be ye not unwise, but understanding what the will of the Lord is. And be not drunk with wine, wherein is excess; but be filled with the Spirit.

2.  **Acts 2:1-4** — And when the day of Pentecost was fully come, they were all with one accord in one place. And suddenly there came a sound from heaven as of a rushing mighty wind, and it filled all the house where they were sitting. And there appeared unto them cloven tongues like as of fire, and it sat upon each of them. And they were all filled with the Holy Ghost, and began to speak with other tongues, as the Spirit gave them utterance.

3.  **Acts 4:8** — Then Peter, filled with the Holy Ghost, said unto them, Ye rulers of the people, and elders of Israel.

4.  **Acts 4:31** — And when they had prayed, the place was shaken where they were assembled together; and they were all filled with the Holy Ghost, and they spake the word of God with boldness.

5.  **Ephesians 5:18-21** — And be not drunk with wine, wherein is excess; but be filled with the Spirit; speaking to yourselves in psalms and hymns and spiritual songs, singing and making melody in your heart to the Lord; giving thanks always for all things unto God and the Father in the name of our Lord Jesus Christ; submitting yourselves one to another in the fear of God.

6.  **1 Corinthians 12:13** — For by one Spirit are we all baptized into one body, whether we be Jews or Gentiles, whether we be bond or free; and have been all made to drink into one Spirit.

## GREEK WORDS

No Greek words were shown in the program in this lesson.

## SYNOPSIS

The baptism in the Holy Spirit is the second work of God's grace, and it is for everyone! (*See* Acts 2:39.) While *peace* is the byproduct of salvation, *power* is the byproduct of the Spirit's baptism. When you are baptized in the Spirit, the "tongue" of your human spirit is loosed and given a voice. That voice is called *speaking in tongues*, and it is natural for every Christian to speak to God in this heavenly language, which bypasses the mind and communicates directly with God, spirit to Spirit.

Jesus said, "God is a Spirit: and they that worship him must worship him in spirit and in truth" (John 4:24). The deepest, most intimate level of worship and communion with God is from *your* spirit to *His* Spirit. This is made possible through the baptism in the Holy Spirit, and God desires this infilling to be an ongoing experience for you, providing you with a steady, abundant supply of His power and many other benefits.

**The emphasis of this lesson:**

**There is one salvation, and there is one initial baptism in the Holy Spirit. These are the first and second works of grace, respectively. After you are initially baptized in the Holy Spirit, there are countless additional infillings you can receive. When you are continually filled with the Holy Spirit, you naturally come under the Spirit's control.**

# Why Do People Drink Alcohol?

There are so many Christians who are wanting to know the "will of God" for their lives, and while there certainly is a specific will God has for each of us, there is also a *general will* that applies to all believers. This general will can be found throughout Scripture, and it includes instructions like we find in Ephesians 5. Writing under the inspiration of the Holy Spirit, the apostle Paul said:

> **Wherefore be ye not unwise, but understanding what the will of the Lord is.**
>
> **— Ephesians 5:17**

In that verse, we are admonished to be wise and understand the will of God for our life. Interestingly, in the very next verse, Paul begins to tell us clearly a big part of what God's will is. He said:

**And be not drunk with wine, wherein is excess; but be filled with the Spirit.**

**— Ephesians 5:18**

Before we unpack the meaning of this verse, we need to ask the question: *Why do people drink wine and hard liquor?* Is it because they just like the taste? Or is there something else at play? The truth is that for many, reaching for a drink is their way of coping with having a hard day. They drink to forget about their problems and to "feel" better.

Others drink to loosen up, free their inhibitions, and cope with the anxieties and fears of life. Still others drink alcohol because they want to have a good time and forget about their troubles. Some drink to anesthetize or escape the pain of the past. Ultimately, the reason most people drink alcohol is because they like the effects it provides.

When people drink, they come under the influence of alcohol, which, ironically, is often called "spirits." Drinking makes them feel different, and they talk and act differently — especially when they're drunk. It's the effects or "buzz" of that altered state that they want to experience. The truth is that when most people begin to drink, they don't even like the taste of alcohol, which is probably because our body was not made to consume it. To like alcohol, most people have to develop a taste for it.

Friend, as a follower of Christ, you don't need to develop a taste for alcohol because you don't need that kind of "spirit" — you have the Holy Spirit! Ephesians 5:18 explicitly says to not be drunk with wine, which in Greek literally means *don't be intoxicated.* The wording here is a strong prohibition, which could be translated, "Don't be intoxicated! Stop it and stop it now!"

# God Wants Us To Be Filled With His Holy Spirit

Instead of instructing us not to be drunk, Paul said, "…Be filled with the Spirit" (Ephesians 5:18). The fact that being filled with the Spirit is juxtaposed with the command not to be drunk tells us that being filled with the Spirit is also going to have an effect on you. So rather than desiring the effect of alcohol, which is fleeting and unhealthy, Paul said to leave the alcohol alone and be filled with the Spirit.

Interestingly, just as verse 17 is connected with verse 18, verse 18 is also connected with verses 19-21. In other words, being filled with the Spirit

(v. 18) is directly linked with the actions we are instructed to carry out in the verses that follow.

> **Speaking to yourselves in psalms and hymns and spiritual songs, singing and making melody in your heart to the Lord; giving thanks always for all things unto God and the Father in the name of our Lord Jesus Christ; submitting yourselves one to another in the fear of God.**
>
> **— Ephesians 5:19-21**

If you are speaking psalms, hymns, and spiritual songs, as well as singing and making melody in your heart to the Lord, that is not natural — it's supernatural. Likewise, if you are submitting to one another in the fear of the Lord, you are definitely under some kind of influence! Something has happened to you that has changed your attitude, your actions, and your perspective. According to Ephesians 6:18, this is the "inebriating" effect of being filled with the Holy Spirit.

# What Happens When We Are 'Under the Influence'?

When people get drunk, they behave differently. In fact, many who are intoxicated become some of the happiest people you'll ever meet while they're "under the influence." They're full of smiles and laughter, they sing songs, and sometimes they even dance. The point is, they are very demonstrative and do things they would never do naturally because they are under the influence of alcohol. There are even some who get drunk and see visions of things that aren't really there.

Paul said that rather than go the route of getting drunk to alter your state of mind, there is a far better alternative: "...Be filled with the Spirit" (Ephesians 5:18). When you are filled with the Spirit, the Spirit will change you, but the influence you come under will have positive, divine effects that are long-lasting.

Instead of being in an angry rage or in a silly stupor where you say and do things you later regret, you will be in a positive mood because you are speaking to yourself in psalms, hymns, and spiritual songs. When you're filled with the Spirit of God, you come under the inebriating effect of the Holy Spirit, and His presence and power operating in and through you will produce great changes.

If you've ever been around individuals who are filled with the Spirit, you know how they can be transformed from a docile person to a demonstrative person. Likewise, people under the influence of the Holy Spirit can also have their eyes opened to the spirit realm, enabling them to see visions and things in the spirit that they wouldn't normally be able to see. Indeed, everything changes when you come under the influence of the Holy Spirit — and it changes for the better!

## Refills Are Free!

Looking once more at the two works of God's grace, the first work is salvation, which brings peace. It is a distinct experience that happens once in a person's life. Similarly, the second work of grace is the baptism in the Holy Spirit, and while this, too, is a once-in-a-lifetime experience, you can be filled again and again and again for the rest of your life.

Again, Ephesians 5:18 says:

> **And be not drunk with wine, wherein is excess; but be filled with the Spirit.**
>
> **— Ephesians 5:18**

The word "filled" here in the original Greek describes an *ongoing action*. Thus, it would be better translated *be being filled continually*. This means that although we receive the baptism in the Holy Spirit once, after that initial experience of speaking in tongues, we can be *refilled* again and again and again. There is actually no limit to how many refills of the Spirit we can each receive. This is a pattern clearly demonstrated in the book of Acts.

## Early Church Believers Were Baptized in the Spirit and Then Refilled With the Spirit Many Times

As we noted in a previous lesson, the first time people were baptized in the Holy Spirit was on the Day of Pentecost. This is documented in Acts 2:1-4, where Luke wrote:

> **And when the day of Pentecost was fully come, they were all with one accord in one place. And suddenly there came a sound from heaven as of a rushing mighty wind, and it filled all the house where they were sitting. And there appeared unto them cloven tongues like as of fire, and it sat upon each of them. And**

**they were all filled with the Holy Ghost, and began to speak with other tongues, as the Spirit gave them utterance.**

When these people — 120 in all — were obediently waiting for the promise of the Father as Jesus had commanded them, they were suddenly filled with the Holy Spirit's power and began speaking in other tongues. Again, this happened on the Day of Pentecost and is recorded in Acts 2.

Sometime later, Peter and John went to the temple to pray, and on the way, they healed a lame beggar near the gate called Beautiful. When the crowd saw the miracle that took place, Peter and John seized the opportunity and began to preach the Good News of Jesus. Infuriated by their actions, the Sadduccess and the temple guards arrested Peter and John and threw them in jail.

When Peter was placed on the witness stand to give an account of his actions to the Jewish Sanhedrin, the Bible says, "Then Peter, filled with the Holy Ghost, said unto them, Ye rulers of the people, and elders of Israel" (Acts 4:8). It's interesting how this reads in the Greek text:

> **"Then Peter, just then in that moment, being filled with the Holy Ghost, said unto them...."**

What this is telling us is that *after* Peter had been baptized in the Holy Spirit in the Upper Room, he was *refilled with the Spirit* here again as he stood to give testimony before the Jewish leaders. This is another infilling. It is as if he came back to the spiritual gas station for a fresh infilling of the Holy Spirit.

Once the trial was over, Peter and John were released and returned to their group of believers and reported to them everything that took place, including the threats made by the Jewish leaders. Immediately, all the believers began to pray, and the Bible says:

> **And when they had prayed, the place was shaken where they were assembled together; and they were all filled with the Holy Ghost, and they spake the word of God with boldness.**
> **— Acts 4:31**

It's important to note that these were the same believers who were baptized in the Holy Spirit on the Day of Pentecost, which means what took place in Acts 4:31 is *another infilling*. Again, this demonstrates that while there is one baptism in the Holy Spirit, there are numerous refillings. There is no limit to the number of "refills" of the Spirit a person can receive. Those who hunger and thirst for more of the Spirit will be continually filled with more of the Spirit.

## Rick Has Experienced Numerous Fresh Infillings of the Holy Spirit

Just like the believers in the Early Church, Rick experienced the baptism in the Holy Spirit and then multiple subsequent infillings after that. He said:

> I received the baptism in the Holy Spirit on January 11, 1974, and my life was forever changed. I had already been saved when I was a very young man. I still remember walking down the aisle of our Baptist church and giving my heart to Jesus. That same night I was baptized in water, and I received the priceless peace of God. At that moment, I knew without a doubt I was going to Heaven.
>
> Nearly ten years later, I received the baptism in the Holy Spirit, which clothed me with the power of God. Within a few hours, I began to pray in tongues. The Spirit's baptism was a one-time experience, but since that time in 1974, I have been refilled with the Holy Spirit hundreds and hundreds of times.
>
> In fact, I begin every day of my life by praying, "Holy Spirit, refill me with You for what I will face today. I open myself up to You for a fresh infilling. Please give me what You know I need. In Jesus' name."

Regardless of your age or when you got saved, you can have as many new infillings of the Holy Spirit as you desire.

## Frequent Infillings of the Holy Spirit Will Transform You Into a Different Person

Let's return to Ephesians 5:18: "And be not drunk with wine, wherein is excess; but be filled with the Spirit." Again, Paul strongly commanded the believers in Ephesus — and us — to leave alcohol alone and to instead be filled and filled and filled continuously with the Holy Spirit.

Just as alcohol has an intoxicating effect, being filled with the Holy Spirit has a spiritually intoxicating effect. It changes your entire perspective on life, including how you think, how you feel, how you behave, and how you relate to others. The *dunamis* power of the Holy Spirit turns you into a Christian who is energized by and under the control of the Holy Spirit.

As we saw in Ephesians 5:19-21, each fresh infilling is inseparably linked to...

- "Speaking to yourselves in psalms and hymns and spiritual songs, singing and making melody in your heart to the Lord."
- "Giving thanks always for all things unto God and the Father in the name of our Lord Jesus Christ."
- "Submitting yourselves one to another in the fear of God."

Let's face it, apart from the Holy Spirit, we are not very thankful people. In fact, we are prone to faultfinding, grumbling, and complaining about people, problems, and things that don't go our way. These are all natural responses.

But when we are filled and continuously refilled with the Holy Spirit, we are no longer the man or woman we used to be. The more we come under the intoxicating effects of the Holy Spirit, the more we are controlled by the Spirit, and the more He changes us into the image of Jesus.

Under the influence of the Spirit, even when something bad happens, you're able to see the good in it. Despite the challenges you're facing, you're filled with thanksgiving because the fresh infilling of the Holy Spirit is working in you, which changes your outlook. You're able to be joyful and give thanks to God in all things (*see* 1 Thessalonians 5:16,18).

What's more, you are even able to submit yourself to others in the fear of God (*see* Ephesians 5:21). Rather than fight to get your own way and be hard to get along with, when you're continuously filled with the Holy Spirit, suddenly you become flexible, agreeable, and willing to submit to others. The only way to experience this kind of peaceful existence is to be *ever-filled* with the Spirit.

## Learn How To 'Drink' of the Spirit

There is one more verse we want to look at, and it was written by the apostle Paul to the believers in Corinth who apparently were at odds with one another regarding whose gift was greater. To help diffuse the arguments and reunite their hearts and minds, Paul said:

**For by one Spirit are we all baptized into one body, whether we be Jews or Gentiles, whether we be bond or free; and have been all made to drink into one Spirit.**
— 1 Corinthians 12:13

According to this verse, you were fashioned by God to *drink of the Spirit.* In Greek, the word "drink" here means *to fill* or *saturate oneself with.* In this case, we are to fill or saturate ourselves with the Holy Spirit. This is a learned practice in which we begin to seek God, praying in the heavenly language of tongues, and asking the Holy Spirit to not just touch us but to fill us to the full again and again, every day.

Again, the more you drink of the Spirit and are refilled with Him, the more you are under the Spirit's control.

Friend, listen to God's command through Paul and put the alcohol away and anything else that is intoxicating you. You don't need to binge on booze, sex, movies, music, or anything else this world has to offer. All you really need is the supernatural drink of the Holy Spirit. *You were made to drink of the Spirit.* If you will begin to open yourself up daily and say, "Holy Spirit, I'm here to drink of You. Fill me, Jesus, with the Holy Spirit," your life will take on new meaning and purpose!

## QUESTIONS AND ANSWERS WITH RICK RENNER

In the program, Rick answered the following question from one of our viewers.

**Q. Is it possible for a person to be baptized in the Holy Spirit and yet not speak in tongues?**

**A.** That's a great question. When I was first baptized in the Holy Spirit, I didn't speak in tongues immediately because I was afraid. I had to break through some mental barriers, including fear of what others thought of me, before I was fully released and able to begin praying in other tongues.

If you study the New Testament — especially Acts 2 through Acts 19 — you will discover that every single time people were baptized in the Holy Spirit, it was always accompanied by them speaking in tongues. This biblical pattern tells us that if when you are baptized in the Holy Spirit, eventually, you should begin to speak and pray in other tongues.

# STUDY QUESTIONS

*Study to shew thyself approved unto God, a workman that needeth not to be ashamed, rightly dividing the word of truth.*
— 2 Timothy 2:15

1. As you conclude this series, what is your biggest takeaway? What encouraged you most, and what challenged you most? What new aspect(s) did you learn about the Person of the Holy Spirit?

2. According to the original Greek meaning of Acts 4:8, Peter was *refilled with the Holy Spirit* in the moment that he stood to give his testimony before the Jewish leaders. What promise do you have from God that is found in Luke 12:11,12; Matthew 10:19,20; and Mark 13:11?

3. The more you drink of and are refilled with the Spirit, the more you experience His intoxicating effects and come under His influence. Knowing this, take a careful look at Romans 8:1-17, and ask the Holy Spirit to show you what *being filled continually* with Him can look like in your life.

# PRACTICAL APPLICATION

*But be ye doers of the word, and not hearers only, deceiving your own selves.*
— James 1:22

1. When you've had a really hard day or find yourself overwhelmed by the challenges of life, what do you normally reach for to find comfort and strength? If it's anything other than God, pray: "Father, please forgive me for allowing other things to be a substitute for You. Help me seek You first and receive true strength and restoration from Your Holy Spirit. I need You, Lord. Thank You in advance for filling me with Your Spirit. In Jesus' name. Amen."

2. Ephesians 5:18 says, "...Be filled with the Spirit." In Greek, it actually means, "...*Be being filled continually* with the Spirit." How does this meaning expand your understanding of the baptism in the Holy Spirit? How can you be *refilled daily* with the Spirit of God?

3. Thank God, there is no limit to the number of refills of the Spirit a person can receive! Those who hunger and thirst for more of the Spirit will be continually filled with more of Him. Are you content with

your relationship with the Holy Spirit? Would you like to experience more of His empowering presence and grace in your everyday life? Take some time to pray, inviting the Holy Spirit into your life and praying in tongues to strengthen your spirit.

## A Prayer To Receive Salvation

If you've never received Jesus as your Savior and Lord, there's no better time for you to experience the new life Jesus wants to give you. To receive God's gift of salvation through Jesus, pray this prayer from your heart:

*Jesus, I repent of my sin and receive You as my Savior and Lord. Wash away my sin with Your precious Blood and make me completely new. I thank You that my sin is removed, and Satan no longer has any right to lay claim on me. Through Your empowering grace, I faithfully promise that I will serve You as my Lord for the rest of my life. In Your name. Amen.*

If you just prayed this prayer of salvation, you are born again! You are a brand-new creation in Christ! Would you please let us know of your decision by going to **renner.org/salvation**? We would love to connect with you and pray for you as you begin your new life in Christ.

# Notes

# Notes

# CLAIM YOUR FREE RESOURCE!

As a way of introducing you further to the teaching ministry of Rick Renner, we would like to send you FREE of charge his teaching, "How To Receive a Miraculous Touch From God" on CD or as an MP3 download.

How To Receive a Miraculous Touch From God
Rick Renner

CD56

RENNER

In His earthly ministry, Jesus commonly healed *all* who were sick of *all* their diseases. In this profound message, learn about the manifold dimensions of Christ's wisdom, goodness, power, and love toward all humanity who came to Him in faith with their needs.

☑ **YES, I want to receive Rick Renner's monthly teaching letter!**

Simply scan the QR code to claim this resource or go to: **renner.org/claim-your-free-offer**

## Connect

WITH US!

www.ingramcontent.com/pod-product-compliance
Lightning Source LLC
Chambersburg PA
CBHW071642040426
42452CB00009B/1735